Joe Hartt—Left, Barney Visser—Right

JOE HARTT

Joe Hartt spent 8 years serving his country as a Naval Aviator primarily aboard CVA-31, U.S.S. Bon Homme Richard, flying A- Skyhawks with Air Groups 12, 19, and 4. Joe logged thousands of hours of flight time and hundreds of day and night carrier landings. This experience, together with extensive night and instrument flight time subsequent to Navy days, has guided his thinking toward development of improved lighting to aid the critical IFR and VFR transition.

Subsequent to his service with the Navy, Joe joined the IBM Corporation, Data Processing contractors to NASA at the Manned Spacecraft Center in Houston, Texas. From 1967 to 1973, he performed a range of tasks in support of the Apollo and early Skylab programs. These included technical and programming requirements definition, systems integration, computer simulations, and actual mission support. He was Manager, Mission Support, and directly responsible for all computer processing functions within the Real Time Computer Complex (RTCC) of the Missions Operations Control Center during all Apollo missions with the exception of Apollo 17.

Joe was the sole or joint holder of several patents, including the Hypersonic Vertical Take-off and Landing Aircraft, Pneumatic Surgical Hand Scrubber, Stratified Change Chamber and Spark Plug, Skateboard Ice and Snow Runner, and the Light-R-Lite.

Joe Hartt died in 1997.

BARNEY VISSER

In 1967, during the height of the Vietnam War, Barney Visser volunteered for the army draft. After his placement testing he was given an option of attending his choice of safe, prestigious, stateside service academies. Instead he volunteered for active duty in Vietnam. He served with the 173rd Airborne Brigade as a paratrooper for 11 months, from July 1968 until June 1969. He served a total of 21 months.

Since Vietnam, Barney, an entrepreneur, founded and built a series of retail stores which today employ over 2,200 full-time team members.

Barney and his wife, Carolyn, are the parents of 7 children.

NOTE: To avoid confusion in a book written by two authors, it has been less confusing to use I, me, mine instead of we, our, ours. We hope you understand me.

VIETNAM

FRESH, POSITIVE INSIGHTS FOR ALL WHO
SUFFERED LOSS IN THE VIETNAM WAR.

JOE HARTT & BARNEY VISSER

Early reactions to VIETNAM:

VIETNAM will be given to every friend I know who suffered loss in Vietnam. I have already seen it bring resolution to hearts that have been heavy since 1968. Join me in passing it on!
> Bobb Biehl
> Founder/President
> Masterplanning Group International

For years I felt we failed in Vietnam. Now I see Vietnam was not in vain. Lessons we learned can save our children's lives. VIETNAM puts value on all we have lost!
> Karen Kimbel
> Homemaker
> Laguna Woods, California

VIETNAM is a clear positive presentation of the freedoms and benefits every American enjoys today . . . BECAUSE . . . of the Vietnam War!
> Bo Mitchell
> President/Co-Founder
> Touch'em All Foundation
> Denver, Colorado

In many respects, Vietnam was inevitable. The "old style" always provided conventional victory. Once that string was broken, we all could rethink the selective use of power. Kosova and the Gulf War notwithstanding, prolonged conflicts in distant locations will probably not be visited upon our children. Economic wars now replace ideological ones, and communism will never effectively compete again. Vietnam was worth this learning. Thank you, Barney and Joe, for such helpful insights.
> Robert A. Seiple
> Ambassador-at-Large for
> International Religious Freedom
> Washington, D.C.

Our family lived with and served among the beloved Vietnamese people for 28 years. We suffered and sobbed the loss of family and friends during that ugly war that no one wanted. I'll never forget being evacuated that last sad day from the U.S. embassy rooftop. The pages of VIETNAM bring new perspective, solace, sense and significance. VIETNAM is a must-read for anyone seeking answers to the question "Why?"
> Dr. Thomas H. Stebbins
> Missionary/Author
> Fort Lauderdale, Florida

VIETNAM
Hartt & Visser

Premiere Publishing
PO Box 50821
Indianapolis, Indiana 46250
www.vietnaminsights.com

ISBN 0-9664049-9-8

Each of the walls is 246 feet and 8 inches long. They meet at an angle of 125.12 degrees. They point exactly to the northeast corners of the Washington Monument and the Lincoln Memorial. The walls are supported throughout their entire length by 140 concrete pilings driven approximately 35 feet to bedrock. At their vertex the walls are 10.15 feet in height. The variations in color and texture are a result of different finishing techniques, i.e. polishing, honing, and flame treatment.

The names of the first casualties appear on the top of East Panel 1 below the date "1959." The last casualties are listed on the bottom line of West Panel 1 above the date "1975." The names were arranged chronologically and typeset from a computer tape of the official Vietnam casualty list. There is a total of 58,209 names as of Memorial Day 1997.

Each name is preceded (on the west wall) or followed (on the east wall) by a symbol designating status. The diamond symbol denotes that the serviceman's or servicewoman's death was confirmed. The approximately 1,300 men whose names are designated by the cross symbol were in missing or prisoner status at the end of the war and remain missing and unaccounted for. In the event a serviceman's remains are returned or he is otherwise accounted for, the diamond symbol is superimposed over the cross. If a man returns alive, a circle, as a symbol of life, will be inscribed around the cross.

Approximately 2,500,000 people visit each year, making the Memorial the most visited site in Washington, D.C.

The Vietnamese Children's Art

The Vietnamese art shown in this book came from stationery gifted to Barney Visser from a World Vision project in Hanoi, Vietnam. The cards were handpainted by street children who are being cared for and rehabilitated in a vocational shelter. The goal of this shelter is to place these children in a nurturing, supportive environment that helps them become positive contributors in their society.

N C ELROD • HERMAN E
INSON • JOHN H JONES •
CHETT • CLIFFORD T MULL
D WHITE • MOISES A REY
MICHAEL J UNSINN • GE
WHITE • EDGAR W WILLIA
AUBAIN • DARRYL V BARN
CHARLES J CATELLI • RI
SHISER • ALFRED D HILDE
ROSS W LIVERMORE • JA
H PLESS • JOSEPH M RAN
LANDIN • ROBERT J CHAL
DER • DAVID D FOSTER •
R HORRELL • HORACE JO
R PETERSEN • HUBERT SIN
A VANEREM • JOHN E FRA

C O N T E N T S

D E D I C A T I O N

This book
is dedicated
to the "average grunt in the field,"
whose ideas were not "high and mighty."
He was just there to help the Vietnamese people.

WEAVER • PAUL J WILSO
TON • FREDDIE A BONET
M DAVIS Jr • EUGENE L DO
ELLINGSON • DANIEL J H
IAM B ROLLINS Jr • ORMA
MS Jr • STEPHEN W McKIN
ARD A CARLSON • DAVID
R CHRISTENSEN • RONALD
BARRY C KELLENBENZ • L
RELAND • CLARENCE McC
GENE L SCHUKAR • DON
LEGRE SUAREZ • THOMA
OTIS KENNEY • FRED D
IN • TERRY LYNN MARTIN
ROY F PHILLIPS • NORMA
WARREN L SPINK • RONA

FRESH INSIGHTS
INTO THE
VIETNAM WAR

Like hundreds of thousands of others within this generation,
my life, plans, and hopes were
interrupted
by an event which most of us have tended to look back upon with
puzzlement,
frequently with deep resentment, all too often with shame.

More than enough of us who participated in it don't care
to look back at all,
choosing rather to seal off those often painful memories
and get on with the business of our lives.

The sad fact, however, is that this event, the Vietnam War,
continues
to this day to affect the lives of thousands of those who fought there.

BY · RUSSELL H ELLIS · JO

ACH · JOHN M LAMANN

UNA · TOM R MUELLER · N

B ROSE III · GEORGE SAN

MES H WARD · JAMES L W

BOYER · RICKY C BRADLE

T A DAVENPORT · EDMON

FELD · WILLIAM E FINLEY

CHARLES J GIBILTERRA Jr

DAVID F HEISER · DOUG

E E JACKSON · RANDALL

LARRY W NEILL · ARTHU

ROMERO · PAUL C RUDY

JOHN J SENOR · KENNE

A TRESSLER Jr · JAMES B

ISIAH BARNES Jr · RON

About 58,000 Americans fell in the fighting.
But
to the final body count must be added
the estimated 100,000 — 200,000 suicides
which have grimly followed in the years since combat ceased.

For my part,
the personal confusion, distress, and quest for understanding
have led me in a different direction.
What, I have asked myself, was the real objective of our war,
the Vietnam War?
What were we Americans really trying to do there?
And above all,
why?

The answers to these simple questions
have for me
become much more remote and difficult to dig out
than one might suspect,
for we now understand that perhaps more than any other war in history,
the entire texture of the Vietnam War
was characterized
by levels of official lying, cover-ups, and intentional deception
within the top posts of our military organizations,
and even more distressing,
at the very highest levels of
our government.

VIS · DAVID O SULLIVAN
· JOHN E BOHNSACK ·
MP · CLARENCE W DUN
ON · ALVIN J HO · RICHA
NNIS C NORTH · HUBER
Y · HAROLD R TYSON · I
ELLS · FRED D WHITAKE
N · THOMAS J CASEY Jr ·
IAM H FARVOUR · EARL
PHILL · ERIC A FISHER · V
EE MILLER · JERRY L MOO
D ROGERS · JOHN S PINN
AROLD J VAN WINKLE Jr
RUNN · MICHAEL A CLU
JLAVIK · HAROLD H HLA

Frustrations
brought about by difficulties in tracking down the truth about
the Vietnam War
led to another search,
this one in many ways even more fascinating and rewarding
than the original.
I began to ask myself:
> So what about the concept of war itself?
>> Why do we fight wars?

>> What is the function of war, anyway?

This question
directed my thinking far back into human history
and
led to an entirely unexpected conclusion.

AM R McNELLY · MICHA
KS · DENNIS W SYDO
N C WOOD · THOMA
OGG · RALPH J GREER
ER · PATRICK E McGOV
RENZO TUGGLE · JOHN
GLEY · ALBERT D BENSO
NA · THOMAS R COLLIN
N · LARRY H JOHNSON
MIS · JERRY W SPEARS
· RUSSELL C NICOLAI
S · THOMAS J ZELENKA
· HAROLD A COX · RO
· DEWEY W HEROY · D

HISTORICALLY SOCIETIES HAVE BEEN HELD TOGETHER BY EXTERNAL THREAT

Human society has always been a matter of life and death,
and war
has always been society's best means for demonstrating this fact.
At its core,
human society requires
that its participants exchange
freedom for survival,
individual rights for the right to be a part of the tribe or family
and
sit with others around the fire for warming and sharing the venison
to stave off starvation.
But
when called upon to defend the tribe or family,
then war it is
which most starkly defines the life and death foundation
upon which human society is structured.

D DENTON • STEPHEN D

N R GAINER • PETER J GE

WS • BRIAN G PARROTT

RLES M SIKES • CURTIS D

• HERMAN WHITE Jr • M

DANIEL A BOLDUC • PER

• STEPHEN D GLECKLER

ERT J KEIN • FRED M KER

L LEWIS • MELVIN LOYD

O CARRASQUILLO SOL

RIS E SHAW • HENRY EST

TRELL • WILLIAM T POC

TONY HARPER • CORN

WILBERT E JONES • ANG

HAROLD O STUMP • S

THE BANANA TREE STORY

Picture the banana tree which can support one family.
All is well.
Although that family will join to protect its tree,
anybody from the family can pick a banana anytime it happens to ripen.
The tree grows
and begins to yield more fruit than the one family needs.
Bananas are falling to the ground and spoiling.

⊢ WILBERT E JONES · AN
KY · HAROLD O STUMP
OSHEIMER · + MICHAEL P
ARDIN · ROBERT A HOFF
O R NILES · RANDY LEE C
SON Jr · JOHN L BRADF
RD K DE FRIES · JAMES L
ALTHERS · HAROLD D W
· WILLIAM E CAMPBELL
· DAVID E FITZGERALD
STICE · RICHARD K LEW
E · DAVID C O'CONNO
SHOOK · JAMES S STAC
O VERA · CARL R WARD
W BLAKE · DENNIS M

A second family observes, circles in, and eventually
works out an arrangement with the first family
that could go something like this:

> Family #1 picks bananas on Mondays, Wednesdays, and Fridays.
> Family #2 picks on Tuesdays, Thursdays, and Saturdays.
> Nobody picks on Sundays.

And as a bonus,
Family #2 will help Family #1 to
protect their mutually beneficial banana tree.
Both families agree to this arrangement,
and the foundations for human society are already subtly visible.
For in making this pact,
Families #1 and #2 have
agreed to
surrender certain freedoms
in return for
ensuring the availability of food for survival.

Consider our own experience at a traffic light.

> When it's green, we go;
> when it's red, we stop.

We have agreed to restrict our absolute freedom
to proceed
in order to
avoid
the prospect of being hit or hitting someone
or of getting a traffic ticket.

FORD · FRANCIS B GA
· JERRY W HILL · CHRIS
OSEPH H MUSSELMAN
APARELLO · CLYDE E PH
EMSEK · JAMES D SPILL
ORDON J TURPIN Jr · JA
GHT · DAVID R BAKER
· JAMES M EARLY · DE
MICHAEL J HAVARD ·
NIEL J KIRCHGESLER · C
EN · EUGENE L MILLER
LUIS E QUINTANA-SO
VILLARD D RICHARDS
BERG · MICHAEL T BOA

But
back to the banana tree.
Say there is not one tree, but an entire grove of them,
sufficient to sustain many families,
an entire tribe.
Now we see an extension of the principle,
though more complex.
The problem becomes,
how does the tribe accurately identify their membership?
Who is entitled to pick and survive,
and
equally important,
who is obligated to defend?

Many tribes resolved this matter by
marking their bodies in some unique way —
curved scars on the forehead,
stripes scarred onto the cheeks.
We've cleaned up the process a little by
moving the stripes onto a piece of cloth which we call a flag,
to which we pledge our allegiance.
But the principle of identification is still there,
and we tend to view ourselves as
members of the American Tribe when marching under that flag.
Certainly the flag carries all the non-subtle implications
of life and death within our society.

SULLIVAN · DAVID L TEICH
HATTEM · JOHN D WALKER
· RONALD L DUCOMMUN
ZKE · VICTOR M GUERRERO
T KASTNER · JOHN M ROSA
N RICARDO W REGALADO
LIAMSON · ADAM WILSON
EL L BILES · PHILIPPE B FALES
D · ROBERT E KUSHMAUL Jr
D RANKIN · DARYL J RUPKE
WN · MARK W BURCHARD
1 CONE · GEORGE J FUERST
JUNGA · THOMAS K KAMP
RINO · DUANE K PETERSON
ROGERS Jr · JAMES F ROST Jr
ARJO · JULIUS ZAPOROZEC
OULDIN · OSCAR L GRIFFIN
SDALE · ROBERT J SCHARES

And here we begin to note an interesting phenomenon:
the warrior kingdoms of ancient China
who were always threatening
or
being threatened from without
were the most successful;
Greece at its peak was threatening
or
successfully dealing with external threat;
Rome was never stronger
nor
better structured than when expanding its borders.

Short, then, of a disastrous collapse of external defenses
leading to the collapse of the society itself,
it seems clear from history that
external threat tends to strengthen the society;
lack of external threat tends to weaken it.
Why should this be?
What is it about external threat that could actually strengthen a society?
The answer seems to be that
external threat reminds the society of its life and death foundation,
and thereby
achieves new power to bond that society.

Vietnam proved
that we can never fight a prolonged war
without an external threat
to our own survival as a society.

GE P McCLINTIC · JAMES
INGTON · GLENN WASH
BOOTH · EDWARD L BO
M · RAYMOND ORITIZ N
S · DAVID J TRBOVICH ·
MIE D BROWN · PAUL E
D L GOODMAN · ROBERT
M RATTIN · MICHAEL K
R · MICHAEL E COTES · M
S STUEWE · LEONARD
LA COMBE · PAUL L MAR
· JOHN H TAYLOR · WAY
L DAWES · GERALD J G
HWICK · PETER J MOLDE
BERT L THANE · EDDIE L
EN H ALLISON · DENNI

4

ONLY THREE SOCIETIES HAVE SUCCEEDED WITHOUT
EXTERNAL THREAT

So now the question arises:
Have there been
or are there today any successful societies
that have survived for any length of time without external threat?
My search has yielded three.

Alexander the Great's Empire lasted for about 150 years
without major wars,
partly because of the brilliant marriage and trading compacts
which Alexander and his staff managed to work out and enforce.
But
after that relatively brief period had passed,
the empire quickly dissolved once more into the smaller,
more familiar,
and much more manageable units which could then return
to the old external threat model
which had worked so well in the past
and which would survive to this very day.

RUS · CALVIN W MAXWE
TRERAS SALINAS · HARR
ERT FLORES Jr · MOSES L
O YBBARA GARCIA · ALAN
K W KINKAID Jr · BERNA
R MIEDZIELEC · ABRAHA
N · WILLIAM ORTEGA Jr
IES R DUFAULT · ROBERT
I LENDERMAN · RICHAR
LO · JOHN T BAKER · JOH
LD C EDWARDS · THOM
L McCLOUD · DONALD
· WILLIAM S SHADE · JC
N W BENNETT · DENNIS
LANNY M HAMBY · JERR
EORGE R McCLINTIC

Next,
the Inca Empire, which arose around 1021 A.D.
and went on to swallow up most everything around it.
By the early to mid 1400s the Inca Empire spread
over about one-third of what we know as South America.
The vast kingdom had run out of enemies.
And until
its disastrous civil war between the royal brothers Huascar and Athualpa
just prior to the arrival of the Conquistadores in 1533,
it was a society substantially without significant external threat.

But
here we note the appearance of an interesting phenomenon.
Within a generation or two of the completion of the Inca conquests,
the ritual of human blood sacrifices was elevated to
top priority and honor.
Time had come to remind the society of its foundations,
and if external threat were not present to accomplish this,
then the high priests were at hand to step in and
perform the reminder rite.
Legend and ancient blood stains
appear to agree
that in one of the great stadiums,
priests stood in blood to their ankles as they opened
the chests of young warriors and ripped out their hearts
to be held up to the sun and to the Inca.
Serious reminder.

AYNES + GERALD R HEL

RONALD G LAUDERDA

SHER · LIONEL E PARSON

NNIS W ROSS · WILLIAM

L TUCCI · BRUCE E WAL

R · RALPH R EVILSIZOR ·

LLIARD · JAMES M MOO

URNER · STEVEN T SCHO

N · TERRY LEE ANDRESEN

N III · RONALD G DE WE

HAGLUND Jr · JOHN A H

ES R LINDSAY · JOEL A M

L STEVENS · EDWARD E

MPSON · RUSSELL E UPR

DEE OKEY N CANAD

Examining the Inca model,
then, as a society which lasted on without serious external threat,
what can we learn about the defining characteristics of such a society?

1.   It was an absolute totalitarian monarchy.
2.   The Inca owned everything.
3.   The Inca was god.

In every practical sense,
the Inca embodied the three tap-roots of society —
politics, economics, and religion.
For most of us, there isn't much about this model of society
that we would find appealing today.

The third example
of a society which has existed for hundreds of years
pretty much without the external threat of war is still going today.
Eskimos have a remarkably war-free history.
But
a cursory examination of their society makes it clear that
while they may not be externally threatened by war,
they constantly face external threat in the form of nature,
a threat real enough and serious enough
to remind them of the essential life and death nature of their society.
Outside of it they face freezing and starvation.
None
could realistically expect to make it on their own.

A SMITH • CALVIN L JO
W WOODY • MICHAEL L
N-ORTIZ • JERRY D DENN
• KENNETH R GODWIN
PAUL H CARDENAS Jr • R
PARTRIDGE • O'NEIL J P
LL • WILLIAM H SMITH Jr
N JAMES C CARMAN • C
FORD • MARK A FOSTER
• RAYMOND N PELKEY
OSE ANGEL SANTA CRUZ
N • BARRY LEE ARMSTRO
ND • WILLIAM E FOLLON
K KIRKBY • DOUGLAS L
H MILLER • GIRAUD D M

So,
aside from our Eskimo society,
we are left with a history that has relied heavily
upon the element of external threat to force the ultimate exchange
of personal freedom for survival.
And which has most readily demonstrated
the life and death nature of that personal exchange
in the function of war.
For the society has always demanded
and
has always received the absolute commitment
of its members to the defense of their
"homeland,"
"flag,"
"way of life," and
interestingly enough,
"freedoms."
This term is particularly significant
in that freedom to fly and escape imminent death is not a option.

LIN · JAMES R GORE · DA
OST · JAMES W LENZ · HA
CHARLES W McLAUREN †
· DONALD A ROWLEY †
YNE R ANDERSON · GEOI
EL R DADISMAN · ALBAR
M · RUSSELL E SLOUGH
ER · CARLOS CHAVEZ Jr ·
NE MATTINGLY Jr · DALE
· MARVIN D SNIDER · DA
LLIAM J CARIVEAU · JERRY
NDRESS · GARY L FLECK ·
ST G HIGHLAND Jr · MELV
DAVID J MOYLAN · STEP
VALLACE ROBERTS · EARL
STEVEN L HIENSMAN · JC

And of course,
each of us who has served our country has taken the oath
which, in effect, says
it's OK to hang a target over our heart
and for the enemy to take his best shot.
For its part,
society says that if the enemy succeeds in that shot,
then the society is pledged to insure that our seed survives —
a pension for the widow
and
children.
With this reassurance, we have willingly gone to war.

GORDON G ANDERSON
OWN · LEROY C CECH · R
EN · BARRY K WEAVER · D
MART · ROBERT F STEELE
DD · WILLIAM R BONNER
DESOCIO · DAVID G DO
RRIL HOLT · FREDERICK W
A PARKS · ROBERT L PORT
· DENNIS M STOPPLEWO
ARNER · DENNIS A LA DAC
HEIT · MICHAEL S BEZEGA
CISNEROS · RAUL DE JESUS
W GUMBERT Jr · CHARLES
McTAGGART · JIMMIE L CH
ILLIAMS · DANIEL K WILSO
E BURNS · NEWTON S CLI

5

SINCE NUCLEAR WEAPONS
WE NO LONGER HAVE THE POSSIBILITY
OF ALL OUT-WAR
WITHOUT SELF-DESTRUCTION

This model seems to have worked remarkably well throughout the ages.
Up until 1945, when a completely new element
exploded onto the scene of human society.
The advent of nuclear weapons
suddenly vaporized
the entire concept
of war and forever altered the function which it had been expected to perform.
Suddenly,
particularly with the quick and inevitable spread of these weapons,
the option of external threat became untenable,
for threatening
and
threatened became one and the same.
No longer could you expect to burn down your enemy's society
without seeing your own go up in flames.

ILLIAM G MARTIN · SAMUE
P PELLEGRINO + MICHAEL J
AVE W BRANT · JOHN P CO
· DANNY V SCURF
· HAROLD W BUTTZ · STEP
· GARY J PALMER · HARI
AMES A CROWLEY II · RICHA
· GLENN S MILLER · DALE
ORGE A VANDERHOFF Jr · RC
· JOHN R FERRAZZANO ·
THOMAS L McKINZIE · SIDN
· JOHN C YATES · B
Y D BENNETT · RICHARD O
· WAYNE J BENES · DANIE
BERT C LANGENHORST · AN

This concept came to be known as MAD, Mutually Assured Destruction,
hardly a reassuring term to any society.
It now appears that we approached this bleak prospect in 1962,
during what history calls the Cuban Missile Crisis.
And
to the everlasting credit of all who made those profound decisions,
human society managed to back away
from the precipice.

But old habits die hard.
How can we really expect in one single generation
to renounce and abandon the old models
upon which human society has rested for virtually its entire history?
War
has always held the stellar place of honor and dignity.
Testimonials abound everywhere.
Witness our proud wearing of the old uniforms,
the ribbons,
medals.
Witness the lofty statues,
memorials,
naming of parks and famous battlefields.
These have been
and continue
to be held as important, even sacred, within our society and those of others.

AUCCI • GERALD L HAM

S • MARK S HAILEY • WI

ROBERT J MUELLENBAC

LASQUEZ • GARY G WI

RODNEY G JOHNDRO

K • RONALD E SAMUEL

AWFORD Jr • GORDON

D M SEYMORE • RALPH

C KAPPMEYER • THOM

IARLIE • DAVID L CLIME

S D MOLES • CALVIN W

M SCANLON • GARY D

E WALSH Jr • PONDEXT

L BAXTER • SHAWN G

MADDUX • ANTHONY

And if the old symbols still command respect and deference,
can it be so surprising that we elected to fall back upon,
at least once more, the old order?
It seems almost inevitable
that sooner or later,
the old order had to be tested,
if only to see whether or not there was still any merit to the concept.
Thus it can hardly be surprising
that our national leadership elected to undertake a war in the old style,
one that we have come to know as
the Vietnam War.

While it is true that the Korean War intervened
between World War II and the Vietnam War,
there were major and fundamental differences
between the two which bear noting.
The Korean War was in both participation and support
an action of the United Nations
which pitted the rest of the world
against North Korea, China, and the U.S.S.R.
Furthermore,
the world in general recognized the North Korean move south
as outright aggression which ought not be tolerated.
After considerable bloodshed and expenditure of munitions,
the territorial issue was ultimately settled
at the original
38th Parallel border.

SMITH • JAMES R TEFFS •
ON • JAMES R FORTENBE
HINES • EDWARD J LAKW
• WILLIAM D BOTHWEL
EIGH • LLOYD H GRIMES
S PIPPINS • CARROLL S P
• THOMAS M BARNETT •
ESCHER • DONALD D CR
EFE • ERNEST H LAIDLER •
NTER Jr • JOSEPH A SILVA
NGMAN • MICHAEL L BR
UPKIN • EUGENE BEAN J
F RONGA Jr • JEFFREY M
M B HERN • DAVID M HO
YUKI • LEONARD W KNC
WARD R McCARTHY III

6

NOT ONE SINGLE COUNTRY
HAS FALLEN TO THE COMMUNIST DOCTRINE
SINCE VIETNAM

Vietnam,
on the other hand,
was a war entered into by the United States Government
for purposes which were never that clearly defined.
Most of us
who were in service at that time were told
that we were fighting this war
to stop the spread of Communism in Southeast Asia.
There was the Domino Theory —
If North Vietnam were to succeed in taking over South Vietnam,
then one by one
the rest of the nations of the area
would in turn choose a Communist form of government.
And while history has proven how hollow this theory was,
at the time it had a ring of authenticity about it,
one which was vitally important to the one actually doing the fighting
in order to give some reason
for the sacrifice he was making for his country.

N • RONALD L HUXTABL
BAKER • JOE MAC BROW
RD L REYNOLDS • LAWR
RY D LAWRENCE • MILA
H MILLER Jr • ROY C OLG
GER D OVERWEG • GARY
R BUSICK • FRANCO DI
GNE • ANTHONY J GALLI
ON • MICHAEL T LINVILL
HAEL L McVEY • JOE PEN
Jr • WILLIAM J HODGES
W GREBBY • DAVID L HIC
B SANDERS • STEPHEN T
NNADY • WILLIAM S DAV
B KIMBROUGH • NATAL
SMITH • JAMES R TEES

So in a very real sense,
it can be said that the Vietnam War was one which was fought over ideas,
rather than territories
or
rights to land per se.
It's important to remember that the Vietnamese Regular
and
the American Soldier were never really fighting the same war.
His was a continuation of the war which the Vietnamese had been waging
for years against a string of invaders —
Chinese, Japanese, French, and finally, the Americans.
He was fighting for his homeland.
And although he failed to win a single decisive battle,
for reasons we all know and understand,
America chose not to exercise its full power and withdrew.

What about our war,
the war of the American Soldier?
Ours was a war of ideas and idealism.
We were told we were over there to stop Communism
from taking over Southeast Asia.
As we look at today's reality,
an interesting question comes to mind:
how many nations in Asia,
or in the entire world for that matter,
have gone Communist since the Vietnam War?
Look at the reality which now prevails in Vietnam itself.

BERT H WILSON Jr · WIL
N A HAMM · WILLIAM A
ILEY D STRUBLE · JAMES
HT · DENNIS H DALE · A
ON Jr · MARION E MEE
IS L ZIEBARTH · JAMES I
OHN R MUCCI · RICHAR
TON · ROBERT L HUDSO
HAEL T MARTIN · ROGER
· ROBERT C RUNGE · EL
EIT · DAVID A BRYAN · V
ROBERT C GOTTIER · PA
ALEY · ROBERT D PERRY
MICHAEL N HUGHES · F
NTT · EDWARD D BURKE

But
the form which this war of idealism took in Vietnam was
the classic model for winning land and territories.

> Saturation bombing,
> rocket attacks on targets of opportunity,
> strafing of troops.
> Rifles,
> hand grenades,
> howitzers.
> River gunboats.
> Patrols.
> Sweeps.
> Campaigns.

All brought forward from the models of war as we have known it,
from antiquity
to its most modern derivatives.
Except,
of course,
any use of nuclear weapons.

This application of classic war technique
to a war of ideals
could only further add to the confusion surrounding the Vietnam War.
While it has been said that
Truth is the first casualty of war,
the Vietnam War was in some respects unique in this regard.
Maj. H. R. McMaster has written a book entitled
Dereliction of Duty in which he makes a strong case
regarding how truth was stifled,
even subverted, during the Vietnam War.

ORGE L JOURDAN-FONT •
Z Jr • DAVID C JAUREGUI
RIDGE • ROBERT J KOLY •
N WARD • EARNEST WILLI
ELMON C CAUDILL II • FR
PHELBON M GREEN • RO
S A JOHNSON III • ROBER
• CHARLES L KOLLENBER
ON H NEWBERRY • DOUC
UES • ROBERT D SCHNEI
RONNIE C TESCHENDOR
ROBERT A BOJANEK • DO
RDS • FREDERICK L FIELDS
OHN C STRINGER II • BEN
ELIPE MORALES • ROGER
RAYNE • THOMAS W FRE

He maintains that instead of carrying out their duties as military leaders,
the Joint Chiefs of Staff
were restrained by President Lyndon Johnson's
"bullying, flattery, and fear of dissent."
They
"became enamored with the trappings of power of the president,"
and
went along with Johnson's deceptions about actual war objectives.

Given this backdrop of confusion
and
outright deception
at the very highest levels of our government
against which the Vietnam War was prosecuted,
it is hardly surprising
that battle commanders in the field
and
the American soldier himself
found the entire experience
in Vietnam
to be embittering and character rending.

M LARRABEE · JOHN C M

Sr · WILLIAM D SMITH ·

· MICHAEL D WRIGHT ·

RIS BROWN Jr · MAXIMIN

OMPSON Jr · OLIN D MA

O · LARRY A SIMONSON

MERIZ PUENTES · JACOB

HUART Jr · WILLIAM A KIN

CE PHILLIPS · JAMES M R

· GERALD ZLOTORZYNS

WILLIE JOHNSON Jr · THO

NE · RONALD J BECKSTED

A BOND · RICHARD R CA

DGEMON · KYLE S HAM

SON · WILLIAM W KIRKPA

To large degree,
the results of the
calculated lying and deceptions hatched
and
propagated from the highest levels of our civil and military government
were borne on the shoulders of the fighting men
who did their best to carry out their orders.

The results of this huge miscarriage of justice
have been disastrous
for Vietnam veterans.
A large percentage have never been able to understand
why they were singled out to bear blame
for something they never understood
and
continue to view with confusion and despair.

WHITE • EUGENE W WICKER
ES E BARNHILL • DEAN A BELL
NION • ROBERT O CHAMBERS
SAMUEL M DEICHELMANN
RAGHTY • GEORGE A GERALD
HARDESTY • DAVID H RISHER
E • RONALD D HUTCHERSON
KELLY • MICHAEL C KOLAROV
LIAMS • ANTHONY J MONTES
SUS OCHOA • EDWIN A PENN
MPSON • EDWARD W SECREST
D L STILL • BRADLEY A St CLAIR
WHELPLEY • DONNIE R WHITE
HT • MICHAEL J ABRUZZESA Jr
DE HAAS • LLOYD D DOERING
H SCHMIDT • ALAN R GERRISH
HORNER • JOHN W JOHNSON
LINGER • ERWIN G POWELL Jr
VIRBERT • STEVEN A WINTERS

Countless tens of thousands have been unable to hold a steady job.
It is estimated that between 100,000 and 200,000
have committed suicide
rather than continue in their personal agony.
Much of this agony stems from a fundamental mismatch
in what they did
as opposed to why they were doing it.
These unfortunate soldiers
could never really understand
the nature of the sacrifice they were being called upon to make
in view of the fact
that the Vietnamese Army
was not
bombing San Francisco
or in any way raising a serious EXTERNAL THREAT
to the folks back home.

P LESANDO Jr • LARRY
OLSON • RANDALL A O
PLUCINSKI • OSCAR K
JON A RIPPEE • ARTUR
RGE J SMITH Jr • JOHN
Y • STEPHEN L TOWNSI
TER • JAMES W WEBB Jr
BARNES • JEFFERY C N
CHAHOC • DELFIN H
DONALD L ELDRID
OLSTON • QUENTIN F
WARD L LAWTON • CH
Jr • JAMES A MORRIS Jr
SHAM I QUICK • PHILI

7

THE KEY ROLE TELEVISION
PLAYED IN THE WAR

For the first time in history,
the realities of war
were seen in the homes of the nation at war,
including those who had given children to fight in the cause.
And while most of what was actually shown was strictly censored
to suit the objectives of the senior officials
who were prosecuting the war,
occasionally a rogue source would bring something approaching reality
to the TV screen,
increasingly so as the war ground relentlessly on
toward no definable conclusion.
These rogue reports were highly distressing,
and
called into question much of the general information
being circulated by the nation's leadership
and
ultimately played a significant role
in bringing about the cessation of hostilities
and
the ultimate withdrawal of American forces.

MOND RODRIGUEZ H
ROWN · CHARLES CLA
USON · RAMON AGUIL
ARDY · HILTON HAYES
ATHANIEL KELLEY · ROY
STEVEN O SCHNELLER
N · KENNETH H SILLS ·
D · HARRY W ANDERSO
N · STEVE J L PERRY · SH
ONG · PIERCE MALMQU
E C PRICE · CHARLES H
AR SOARES · LYN D SPA
ANIEL E WINTERS · WIL
SAMUEL L BOYD Jr · E

8

THE SHATTERING EXPERIENCE OF COMING HOME

But nothing
could prepare the Vietnam veteran for
the shattering experience of coming home again
to the disapproval,
ridicule,
even hate of many of his fellow citizens,
often enough from members of his own family.
Here we see a nation in shock,
not understanding either the war
or
those who answered their country's call
and did their duty to the best of their ability.
The Americans who fought there returned
to a nation who showed them a face of outright hostility.
Many returning soldiers were booed.
Some were spit upon.
Few were welcomed home as dedicated Americans.
Fewer still as heroes
who had endured a kind of hell in trying to do their duty.
This nation to large degree abandoned its own children.
It puts us in mind of the mothers of Sparta
who would charge their sons as they gave them their shields,

"Come back carrying it or on it, but don't come back without it."

RNEST U GAMELIN Jr · R
MARTIN · CHARLES J PA
· DENIS L SIMONE · EVE
AM · PAUL R DARTT · FR
DAVID L EVANS · ARNOL
TER · JOHN J MORLEY Jr
· RICHARD S RILEY Jr ·
R WILSON · RICHARD M
JAMES M ESPOSITO · EI
O LEBRON-MALDONA
AY Jr · JAMES G SANDEF
ON Jr · DENNIS R TRIPP
BATES · JAN A ELKINS ·
E B HOLLAND · CHARLE
SKOWSKI · ABEL LUNA

9

VIETNAM WAS A WATERSHED EVENT IN THAT IT HELPED US DEFINE WHO WE ARE AS A PEOPLE

Despite
the fact that it was executed under the dark wraps
of perhaps the deepest deceptions and lying of any war in history,
perhaps
even to some degree because of this fact,
the Vietnam War will stand out in history as a watershed event
for many reasons.

HENRY • DENNIS G INIG
GERALD C MULLIN • W
OWELL • ALLAN L SCHM
EIGH • RAFAEL SOLER • J
RLES L ADKINS • CHARL
ANDELL L DOCKSTADER
L • LARRY P BROWN • TE
KE • KAZUTO MORIWAK
L • DAVID L THORNTON
AMES A COPELAND • JO
ERTRICK • MITCHELL L JO
RZYK • MARVIN E LIVELY
VOLZ • RICHARD C WA
AWRENCE DE WITT • RI
FU • ALLEN L LUCAS • HO

A. THERE WILL NEVER BE ANOTHER VIETNAM BECAUSE WE HAVE
   LEARNED THESE PROFOUND HISTORIC LESSONS, NOT JUST IN A
   CLASSROOM BUT ON THE BATTLEFIELD!

As we have noted previously,
it was a war planned
and
executed on the old classical models of ground troops
finding and exterminating the enemy (ancient history)
the best of traditional hand weapons (ancient through modern history)
precision and saturation bombing (World War II).
Fastidiously
avoided
were nuclear weapons.

The circumstances surrounding this withdrawal
and
the humiliations associated with it led to the coining of a new slogan:

"No More Vietnams."

LIE JOE ONTIS · GERAL
VAYNE E SKOLITS · CHA
· MELVIN E THOMPSO
ONALD R WENTZ · KEN
CAMPBELL · DAVID A CA
D R EFIRD · GEORGE V
N · PATRICK R HENDRIC
AYMOND B KYZER · DA
OSTOWSKI · CHARLES
D P SANTORA · PAUL A
VEY · BRUCE R J N SWE
DAVID J WILCOX · JAC
LARK JOHN W COLBE
DIEKEMA · ELMER E FRE
ARIO D GUERRA · JAMES

In its thinnest meaning,
these words could imply, "Let's not lose any more wars."
But
the broader meaning here is truly profound:

>"Let our nation
> and
> humanity end our ancient dependence upon classical war
> as a means to effect the survival of our societies."

The implications
of the latter interpretation are obviously huge,
and
single out that Vietnam was a Watershed Event in Human History.
For if indeed that war,
despite (or perhaps to some degree because of) the lies,
deception, confusion, and heartbreak which it embodied,
accomplished the stunning objective of teaching our society
that classical war no longer works,
then it will have taught us a massive and historic lesson.
In a single generation
our society
will have unlearned thousands of years,
thousands of generations of dependence upon the old war model.

Because
of the Vietnam War
few, if any,
of our sons or daughters will ever have to die in a distant country
fighting a war
against an enemy that is no real threat to us at all!

ALD R CONKLIN • ALEX B
JAMES B DILLARD • WILL
NETH G GREEN • JOHN N
BSTER B JOHNSON • JOH
RBAN • BENJAMIN MELVI
ED J PAUL • RICHARD D R
RUSSO • JAMES T SHEFFIE
ARTHUR L WARNER • ST
A Jr • ROBERT CLOKES • TH
GAGE • JERRY W GLAZE • V
WILLIE G JONES • JEROME
O ORTIZ Jr • GARY LOWE
DONALD R STOLTZ • RIC
BLAIR W TWO CROW • B
• CHARLES J AKINS • M
ECE Jr • NYROON CHAD

B. VIETNAM PERSONALIZED WAR

Several major items can be cited.
First,
this war for the first time personalized war
and
ripped away the mask of depersonalized dog-tag numbers.
Witness the huge anti-war demonstrations
of the late sixties and early seventies,
organized and executed for the most part
by independent-thinking citizens
who were not buying into the general party line propagated
by their own government.

Witness the Vietnam War Memorial —
a wall honoring
by individual name
those who fell in Nam.
True,
a small statue of three American troops,
one an African American,
one a Hispanic,
and one a Caucasian,
was later located some distance from the wall.
But
the men are peering toward the wall,
as though with a premonition
that their names, too, will appear on the grand and solemn memorial
to the men who died
or
remain missing there.

R CRIST • RICHARD G D
AMMERSLA • JOHN R HA
• ROBERT R MASCAREN
PKIN • MORTON H SING
H STROUT • GERALD J S
OWN • NORMAN H CLA
N J GOTT Jr • RONALD L H
AS • KENNETH B MILLHC
LD R REEVES • ROY H SH
DAVID L AERTS • GERALD
BURDICK • THOMAS G D
BEN H IDE • ALTON D KE
VILLIAM J PAHR Jr • NOR
AEL P WALSH • LANNY L
CHARD • GEORGE H BUR

C. THE RULES OF WAR HAVE CHANGED FOREVER

A further accomplishment of the Vietnam War
was its effect
upon the nation's view
of its relationship
to the government and military establishment.
While it was never a widely held objective of the protesters
to "bring down the government,"
there was a widely held objective:
to bring down a particular governmental policy.
In this,
the citizens of this nation were successful.
Thus,
it may be fairly said that the Vietnam War
brought to our society
a new definition of who we are
and what our powers and responsibilities are.

The Russians took note of the American experience in Vietnam,
but
apparently judged themselves capable of succeeding where we had failed.
Their long and dismally unsuccessful military foray into Afghanistan
was patterned along the same classical military lines —
troops on the ground supported by attacks from the air.
Russian losses were high.
Back home,
support for the campaign melted away.
Eventually,
the fighting ceased altogether
when the sobered and bloodied Russians withdrew,
having learned for themselves that the rules have changed.
Their experience
only substantiated
what the Vietnam War
had previously burned into the annals of history of human society:
it is time for us to end our ancient dependence upon classical war
as a means to effect the survival of our societies.

RAY PALMER • ROY ST...
RAYMOND J WEST • JERRY
MAN • FRANKLIN P WILLE
ESTER • GEORGE F JOHN
O'BRIEN • JOHN C ROB
A ABRAHAM TRUJILLO-
H B BIXEL • EUGENE M C
CHNER • MARK E MADSE
E RAMSEY • EARNEST E
EAN F SPAULDING Jr • DA
ARK • RICHARD O FISK •
L KNEECE • ZYGMUNT J
RANDOLPH • JAMES M R
D STUART Jr • JOHN A BI
OWN • NEIL R BURNHAM
TH R CRIST • RICHARD

About ten years later,
in 1985,
Mikhail Gorbachev
was discussing the concept of Perestroika and Glasnost
with the Soviet leadership.
Two years later he announced it to the world.
To some degree at least,
our shared national experiences
in Vietnam and Afghanistan pointed toward Perestroika.
It was past time
for Soviet society to reexamine
their roots of secrecy,
imprisonment for dissident views,
suppression of personal freedoms,
and
above all,
dependence upon a military and police establishment
to make their society work.

AM H PLESS • JOSEPH M
W BLANDIN • ROBERT J C
A FEDER • DAVID D FOS
ALD R HORRELL • HORA
ARL R PETERSEN • HUBER
AN A VANEREM • JOHN E
HENEY • GARY W ARNAU
DAVID L JOHNSON • WA
OGETT • MARVIN C PEDE
RALPH L VOGELI • JOSEPH
OUGH • CHARLIE A DAV
TY • PAUL D FLEMING • A
GLENN E HOBART III • VI
K MERRELL • RONALD L N
LSON • ROBERT V PACK

D. HELPED US UNDERSTAND THE VERY NATURE OF WAR

In today's world,
while many are deeply concerned about their economy
and
the role that we may be playing there,
it would be hard for most Russians to believe
that the United States is out to get them militarily.
By the same token,
power brokers in the United States
no longer even attempt to play off our military powers against
countries who remain Communist.
As we noted earlier,
the spread of that doctrine has come to a virtual standstill.
The general expectation
is that in those few nations (Cuba, North Korea)
who still cling to the discredited ideas,
much of the reason that they do so can be traced to
the strong personalities who dominate their society's political landscape.
The further expectation
is that when these individual personalities are gone,
barring the emergence of an equally powerful successor,
a general overhaul of the society may well take place
which could bring about a more reasonable
and
successful society model.

ELVIN E CLAY • LARRY C
BY • RUSSELL H ELLIS • JC
ACH • JOHN M LAMANN
NA • TOM R MUELLER •
B ROSE III • GEORGE SAN
MES H WARD • JAMES L V
BOYER • RICKY C BRADL
A DAVENPORT • EDMO
FELD • WILLIAM E FINLE
CHARLES J GIBILTERRA Jr
DAVID F HEISER • DOUG
E JACKSON • RANDALL
LARRY W NEILL • ARTHU
ROMERO • PAUL C RUD
JOHN J SENOR • KENNE

It is interesting to note that
substantially all conflicts and wars now flaring around the world
are either religious or economic at their roots.
Far and away the most significant in terms of peoples involved
and
commitment to death
are those conflicts based upon religious differences.
It is significant that in the most recent confrontation between the U.N.
and Saddam Hussein of Iraq,
not a single Arab/Moslem voice has been raised in criticism
of Saddam
or
of his decision to flout the U.N. inspection team mandate
which for years has been understood and accepted by Iraq.

And
the "ethnic purification" which we witnessed
pretty much across the board in the formerly communist nation
of Yugoslavia
in which uncounted citizens died
merely because they were of the "wrong ethnic stock and religion,"
was nothing more than religious passion
out of control.
And while American servicepeople joined their counterparts
from other U.N. nations,
it was understood by everyone involved
that Americans would never allow
another
Vietnam.

Vietnam
forced us to establish the limits
of what we would
and
would not do
in time of war.

ISIAH BARNES Jr · RO
O CASSIDY · THOMAS
NT · GORDON D GAR
SEN · LESLIE A JERSTAD
· MICHAEL S MASSONE
MUSSEN · JOHN R REBIT
MPLE · JOHN T WALLS ·
HAEL A BARNES · ROBER
H BRUBAKER Jr · LEE E B
· ANTHONY A BARBARI
GILDOW · OTIS GREEN
· DAVID HOWZE Jr · C
· ANTHONY L QUINN
GERALD L THOMAS
ALKER · FRANKIE R WIL

10

VIETNAM: WON OR LOST?

While on a recent visit to Vietnam,
I was astonished at the friendliness,
even affection,
which the Vietnamese people showed
when they learned that I had been there as an American soldier.

Why the remarkable friendliness?
Just outside My Lai stands a monument.
It was intended to memorialize
the savage brutality of the American troops who came through,
searching for the Viet Cong
they knew were hiding among the villagers.
To those of us who were there,
it commemorates exactly the opposite.
We, and I now sense that many Vietnamese as well,
view it more as a symbol to the restraint
which our troops exercised
a thousand times for the one terrible venting of frustration and rage
upon My Lai.
These villagers candidly admitted to me
that they were far more terrified of the Viet Cong among them
than of our soldiers,
who,
by refusing to repeat My Lai, became virtual sniper bait for the V.C.

D H HLADIK • DENNIS J

HABER • WELDON G LY

ER • CHARLES E SCHO

ARTHUR L BROWN S

GIL C COMBS • JOHN

RODNEY R GREEN •

E KELLY Jr • MARWICK

SON • RONALD L RAKE

AN Jr • WARNELL E ATE

S W DALTON • GARY R

NS • RICKIE N GUNDER

A KUCICH • CHARLES

POE • RICHARD L WAY

SMITH • ROY D STOFF

ROBERT C WIN

To my own great personal distress
and
to that of most of us who fought there,
for years now it's been said that the Vietnam War was lost,
that it constituted nothing more than a huge waste of
life, time, goods,
and
that from it sprang nothing but the bitter fruit of frustration
and despair and endless suffering of mind and spirit.

Why?
What has driven these good and worthy men to such an end?

My sense of this tragic reality
is that it stems from a deep and deadly guilt
which feeds upon a massive misinterpretation of history,
officially sanctioned
and
accepted for years pretty much without question.
These late casualties are convinced that they lost the War
for their Country.
And given the line of thought which has prevailed,
what else has there been to believe?

Y · LAWRENCE H MOO⌐
CARDO · BILLY D ROBER⌐
O SULLIVAN · JUAN J V⌐
OHNSACK · BENJAMIN⌐
NCE W DUNBAR · JAME⌐
HO · RICHARD R HUR⌐
RTH · HUBERT PALMER⌐
R TYSON · LEWIS R VA⌐
D WHITAKER · WAYNE⌐
J CASEY Jr · THOMAS ⌐
OUR · EARL F HOUCK⌐
A FISHER · VERNON G⌐
JERRY L MOORE · HUG⌐
OHN S PINNEY · NELSO⌐
N WINKLE Jr · ROBERT W⌐

But wait.
Is this the true picture that emerges today
when we take a
step back
to gain a realistic historic perspective of the event?
Was this war won or lost?
And if so, who won, who lost?
It is long past time to end the delusion of a war lost,
and
for a general overhaul of American perception
of this watershed event in history
which we have tended to look back upon with confusion
and
even shame.
We need to open our eyes and end 25 years of nonsense.
Today's reality
testifies mightily that the American sacrifice in Vietnam
not only accomplished its stated objective,
but
that it also moved our culture and society along a pathway
to understanding war
in a far different, less romantic, hard reality sense.

DALBERTO R E VERDU

LISTER Jr · BYRON D Mc

PISIL · WILLIAM E PRICE

DA Jr · RICHARD L SHUG

HOMAS · RONALD T V

ARENCE J BABIN Jr · JEF

Jr · HAROLD D BILLER ·

CHAEL C BURNS · MIC

COMBS · BRUCE W CUI

SAMUEL A EKLOFE · R

ISON · JUAN GASTON

AN · JOHN T HARE · RIO

ND · RODGER D HOLM

N VARGAS GARCIA · RO

ROGER M KITTLESON

Notice.

No more Vietnam Wars.

Our children have not been dying by the thousands

in Rwanda, Uganda, Haiti, Yugoslavia.

Military action often becomes policing action.

How to get food to people left to starve by their own leadership

has now become a major function of military effort

and

responsibility since Vietnam.

We learned,

as did the Soviet Union

in their own crushing experience in Afghanistan,

that war is no longer

the stuff of heroes on horses, monuments, parades and high ceremonies.

As so intensely conveyed by the Vietnam Wall in Washington,

war

must ultimately be viewed as a highly personal act.

Oddly enough,

it was the advent of Nuclear Weapons of mass destruction

which lies at the core of this personalization.

The Vietnam War became our teacher and our conscience.

It gave us definition of who we are.

LANCIOT • DONALD

N • DAVID A MALLORY

RT A McCARTHY • THO

PARKER • JAMES D PES

SEY • FREDERICK R RAT

OBINSON SANTIAGO •

P SEEL Jr • ALLEN M SH

F SMITH • JOHN M SU

IANT • ROBERT H TRAIL

THOMAS C WARNER •

IGER • JOHNNY G WIL

STEPHEN S NIEDERHA

HRISTOPHER BROW •

E COVINGTON • DAV

DESPER • JIM L DICKSO

It is now time for the pain to end.

Lincoln's words at Gettysburg seem remarkably applicable to Vietnam:

"It is for us the living rather to be dedicated here to the unfinished work which they who fought here have thus far so nobly advanced. It is rather for us to be here dedicated to the great task remaining before us — that from these honored dead we take increased devotion — that we here highly resolve that these dead shall not have died in vain...."

VIETNAM SOLDIERS DID NOT DIE IN VAIN!

In Vietnam today,
the seeds of freedom
and
free enterprise
are taking root and growing.
This, after all,
is what the American Soldier's Vietnam War was all about.

A GRABBE • LOWELL R
LARENCE M HOLLAND
Jr • JOHN W KOBELIN
LOONEY • DAVID G L
ER • JOHN T McDONN
CHAEL L WOODSIDE • L
SEAMAN • PAUL E STRO
GLENN S WINGENBAC
F ANSELMO • ALLEN R A
OWN • MARION M BUR
EORGE • JAY B GILPIN •
MAN • LINNELL BUTLER
OLENC • ADOLF J KRO
ZAL • JOHN H WEST •
AM L McNAMARA • JOS

MY PERSONAL REFLECTIONS ON THE VIETNAM WAR

S L SMITH • RYUZO SO

ADO • EFRAIN FIGUER

CALLAN • MICHAEL A C

MICHAEL A DUNNEBAC

RCIA • HAROLD S GLAD

VARD R HICKEY • EARL

N • SANDERFIERD A JON

D B LANE • DANIEL W LA

NTINE • JOHN A NOWA

ATON • CLAYTON A SO

AS • LESLIE D THOMPSO

ON Jr • GEORGE R AVG

ELDER • WEYMAN T CO

COLEMAN • CLAYTON

LA CRABBE • LOWELL L

My Personal Reflections on the Vietnam War

NOLAN Jr · ROBERT W O
EWSKI · TERRY C SIMISO
AVER · PAUL J WILSON ·
· FREDDIE A BONETTI ·
AVIS Jr · EUGENE L DOTS
NGSON · DANIEL J HOLT
B ROLLINS Jr · ORMAN S
· STEPHEN W McKINLEY
A CARLSON · DAVID C H
RISTENSEN · RONALD L I
RY C KELLENBENZ · LEO
AND · CLARENCE McCRA
E L SCHUKAR · DONALD
RE SUAREZ · THOMAS A
TIS KENNEY · FRED D KES
ERRY LYNN MARTIN · D

SPEECH OUTLINE

VIETNAM SOLDIERS
DID NOT
DIE IN VAIN . . .

1. Historically societies have been held together by external threat.

2. Since nuclear weapons we no longer have the possibility of all-out war without self-destruction.

3. Therefore, the rules of war have changed forever.

4. Vietnam proved that we can never fight a prolonged war without an external threat to our own survival as a society.

5. VIETNAM SOLDIERS DID NOT DIE IN VAIN!

   A. Vietnam was a watershed event in that it helped us define who we are as a people.

   B. Vietnam forced us to establish the limits of what we would and would not do in time of war.

   C. Not one single country has fallen to the communist doctrine since Vietnam.

   D. There will never be another Vietnam because we have learned these profound historic lessons, not just in a classroom but on the battlefield!

   E. Because of the Vietnam War, few, if any, of our sons or daughters will ever have to die in a distant country fighting a war against an enemy that is no real threat to us at all!

ND P KURTIK • FRANK
E NEWELL • JAMES L O
RE • CHARLES E SMITH
T • DANNY K YELLEY • C
SHOP S BARANOWSKI
RLES P CHANDLER • G
ROBERT V GAPINSKI •
RANT • DONALD L GR
S • JOHN D MARTIN • C
ON • HERBERT L PHELPS
E SISLEY • JAMES E SIZ
ELD • THOMAS J BARN
DAVIS • ROBERT DIAKO
GABOOK • ANASTACI

VIETNAM SOLDIERS
DID NOT
DIE IN VAIN . . .

1. Historically societies have been held together by external threat.

2. Since nuclear weapons we no longer have the possibility of all-out war without self-destruction.

3. Therefore, the rules of war have changed forever.

4. Vietnam proved that we can never fight a prolonged war without an external threat to our own survival as a society.

5. VIETNAM SOLDIERS DID NOT DIE IN VAIN!

   A. Vietnam was a watershed event in that it helped us define who we are as a people.

   B. Vietnam forced us to establish the limits of what we would and would not do in time of war.

   C. Not one single country has fallen to the communist doctrine since Vietnam.

   D. There will never be another Vietnam because we have learned these profound historic lessons, not just in a classroom but on the battlefield!

   E. Because of the Vietnam War, few, if any, of our sons or daughters will ever have to die in a distant country fighting a war against an enemy that is no real threat to us at all!

SPONSORED BY:

YOUR GROUP

AVID P CALLAHAN · GAR
OBERT S DANKERT · DON
N W GREGORY · LOUIE F
HESS · MERLE R HIGGINS
HOWARD · EDWARD E K
Jr · JOHN R MAXSON ·
HAROLD L PARKIN · LA
CHARLES M RAMSEY ·
IAGO Jr · ANTHONY J SE
X TURNER · HUGO H UL
ENSEL · THOMAS J WILLIA
RY H BARBEE · JOHN P BE
RAGG · JOSEPH BRESKI Jr
VENGER · JOHN P CRAIG
MANN · MICHAEL J EVAN
STEPHEN B GEURIN

PASS THE WORD . . .

If you know people
who would find this book comforting, resolving, helpful,
please give them a copy.
Let them read yours . . .
copy a few of your favorite pages . . .
or
buy an extra copy and give it to them.

Help friends heal.
Help them gain a new perspective on the war.
Help them see that the heavy cost they paid was not in vain!

Thank you.

ORDER FORM

PLEASE SEND ME _____ COPIES OF VIETNAM FOR $10.00 EACH
(PLUS $2 FOR POSTAGE AND HANDLING).

My Name (Please Print) _____

Position _____

Organization _____

Mailing Address _____

City/State/Zip _____

Telephone: DAY (_____)_____ FAX (_____) _____

E-mail Address: _____

METHOD OF PAYMENT:

❏ Cash   ❏ Check   ❏ MasterCard   ❏ Visa

Name on Card _____

Card Number _____

Expiration Date (mo./yr.)_____ Order Date _____

Signature _____

ORDERING NOTES:

ORDERING BY PHONE (WITH MASTERCARD OR VISA):

Call Toll Free 1-800-482-6372.

ORDERING BY FAX (WITH MASTERCARD OR VISA):

Fill in all information on the order form and FAX it to 1-317-576-9196 (24 hours).

ORDERING BY MAIL:

Fill in credit card information or make check or money order payable to Premiere Publishing and send orders to:

Vietnam Book
C/o Premiere Publishing
P.O. Box 50821
Indianapolis, Indiana
46250-0821

1. ORDER FULFILLMENT:
Please allow 21 DAYS FOR DELIVERY.

2. Call for Express Delivery.

3. INTERNATIONAL ORDERS: (check one) ❏ AIR ❏ SURFACE
International orders, choose one:
(a) charged to a MasterCard or Visa
(b) check drawn from a United States Bank
(c) International money order — International orders will be put on your credit card at actual postage rates.

ORDERING BY EMAIL:

Supply the information requested on the opposite page and email to orders@vietnaminsights.com or visit the website at www.vietnaminsights.com.

All amounts in U.S. Dollars.

AVID P CALLAHAN · GAR
OBERT S DANKERT · DON
N W GREGORY · LOUIE F
HESS · MERLE R HIGGINS
HOWARD · EDWARD E K
S Jr · JOHN R MAXSON ·
HAROLD L PARKIN · LA
CHARLES M RAMSEY ·
IAGO Jr · ANTHONY J SE
X TURNER · HUGO H UL
ENSEL · THOMAS J WILLIA
RY H BARBEE · JOHN P BE
RAGG · JOSEPH BRESKI Jr
VENGER · JOHN P CRAIG
MANN · MICHAEL J EVAN
D · STEPHEN B GEURIN

THE VIETNAM WAR
REPRESENTS
HEARTRENDING LOSS.

BUT,
IT ALSO REPRESENTS
SUBSTANTIAL HISTORIC GAIN.

YOUR
SACRIFICE WAS MOST CERTAINLY NOT IN VAIN!